The

TIM WALZ

Biography

A Comprehensive Exploration of His Legacy *of*
Service, *Leadership*, and *Resilience*

John Bison

Table *of* Contents

Introduction

In the quiet corners of *Minnesota*, where the vast expanse of the plains meets the *gentle* embrace of the *Mississippi River*, a story began to unfold that would eventually ripple through the corridors of power in *Washington*, D.C. Tim Walz's journey from the heartland of *America* to the high-stakes realm of *national politics* is not merely a chronicle of a career but a testament to the extraordinary power of *dedication*, *resilience*, and *unyielding* commitment to service.

Born in the small town of *West* Point, Nebraska, Tim Walz's early life was steeped in the values of *hard* work, community, and a profound sense of responsibility. The landscape of his childhood—where the sky seemed endless and the rhythm of life was marked by the changing seasons—shaped his *character* and *instilled* in him a deep connection to the land and its people. His experiences growing up in this tight-knit community provided a foundation of empathy and understanding that would later define his approach to public service.

Education played a pivotal role in Tim's life, not just as a formal process but as a *transformative* journey. His time as a *high school* teacher was marked by an unwavering dedication to his students, an appreciation for the power of education, and a commitment to fostering a nurturing learning environment. This period of his life was characterized by a hands-on approach to teaching, where the *classroom* became a crucible for shaping young minds and instilling values of integrity, perseverance, and critical thinking.

The transition from educator to elected official was a significant leap, but one that Tim approached with a blend of pragmatism and idealism. His entry into the political arena was driven by a desire to make a tangible difference in his community, and to translate his understanding of local issues into effective policy solutions. This journey was marked by a series of milestones—each a step toward a broader platform where his voice could resonate on a national scale.

As Tim Walz navigated the complex landscape of American politics, he did so with a clear sense of purpose. His tenure in Congress was characterized by a commitment to addressing pressing issues such as education reform, healthcare, and veterans' affairs. Each legislative *battle* was a reflection of his dedication to improving the lives of others and his belief in the power of collaborative problem-solving. The halls of Congress, with their grandeur and historical significance, became the stage where Tim's ideals and expertise were put to the test.

The nature of Tim's service was not just about legislative victories but about the relationships forged and the *trust* earned. His ability to work across party lines and engage with diverse perspectives was a testament to his commitment to finding common ground and advancing effective solutions. The political landscape of his time was marked by polarization and division, but Tim's approach was characterized by a focus on unity and constructive dialogue.

Personal sacrifices were an *inherent* part of Tim's public life. The demands of his career required long hours, frequent travel, and a significant amount of time away from family. Balancing these demands with personal and familial responsibilities was a constant challenge, but one that Tim managed with a sense of duty and an unwavering commitment to his role as a public servant.

As Tim Walz's story continued to unfold, the impact of his work became increasingly evident. The improvements in education funding, advancements in healthcare access, and enhanced support for veterans were tangible outcomes of his dedication and hard work. These achievements were not just legislative milestones but reflections of a broader commitment to making a positive difference in the lives of individuals and communities.

The horizon of Tim's journey was not confined to the immediate challenges of public service. As he transitioned to new roles and opportunities, his story continued to evolve, marked by a focus on advocacy, consultancy, and personal growth. The lessons learned and the experiences gained during his time in Congress provided a *foundation* for continued impact and influence in various domains.

The narrative of Tim Walz's life is a *rich* tapestry of *experiences, values,* and *achievements.* From his early days in Nebraska to his influential role in Congress and beyond, his journey is a testament to the power of resilience, dedication, and a deep commitment to public service. As the story of Tim Walz continues to unfold, it serves as an inspiration and a reminder of the enduring impact that one individual can have on the world.

Chapter 1

The Seeds of Ambition

In the tranquil embrace of West Point, Nebraska, a tapestry of verdant fields and open skies set the stage for the early years of Tim Walz. Born on April 6, 1964, in this small, tight-knit community, Tim's formative years were shaped by the rhythm of rural life and the enduring values of his family. West Point, with its modest charm and a population where everyone knew each other's name, offered a landscape of both simplicity and profound significance. It was here, amidst the expanse of farmland and the quiet hum of daily routines, that Tim's journey began—a journey that would lead him far beyond the confines of his hometown.

The Walz family farm was a world unto itself, a realm where the values of hard work and perseverance were not merely taught but lived. Tim's father, Jim Walz, was a farmer whose life was a testament to the rigorous demands of agriculture. The farm's rhythm—the planting of seeds in spring, the laborious tending during the summer, and the harvest in autumn—was not just a series of tasks but a way of life. Jim's hands, weathered and strong from years of tilling the soil, spoke of an unwavering commitment to his work and an understanding of the land's subtle cues.

Tim's mother, Darlene, balanced her husband's hard labor with a nurturing presence that created a warm and supportive home environment. Her role extended beyond the domestic sphere; she was deeply involved in community activities, lending her support to local initiatives and fostering a spirit of generosity. The Walz household was a haven of encouragement, where Tim and his siblings learned the values of responsibility, integrity, and the importance of giving back.

From a young age, Tim was immersed in the life of the farm. The sprawling fields became his playground, and the chores of farm life his early lessons in discipline. Mornings began with the sun's first light, casting a golden hue over the land as Tim joined his father in the day's work. The farm was a place of physical exertion and mental fortitude, where each task, whether it was mending fences or tending to livestock, contributed to a larger purpose. These early experiences were formative, shaping Tim's work ethic and his understanding of the importance of perseverance and dedication.

Yet, while the farm life instilled in Tim a sense of responsibility and resilience, it was also a place of joy and discovery. The vast fields offered a sense of freedom, a boundless space where Tim could let his imagination run wild. The simplicity of rural life allowed for moments of wonder—a sudden rainstorm that transformed the landscape into a shimmering canvas, or the quiet stillness of a summer evening under a canopy of stars. These experiences, while seemingly ordinary, laid the groundwork for a deep appreciation of both the natural world and the sense of possibility that lay beyond the horizon.

School in West Point was a small but significant part of Tim's early education. The local schoolhouse, with its familiar faces and close-knit community, provided an environment where every student's potential was recognized. Tim's natural curiosity and enthusiasm for learning set him apart. He was the kind of student who asked probing questions and eagerly absorbed new information. His teachers, attuned to his bright mind and leadership potential, encouraged his academic pursuits, fostering a love for learning that would serve him well in the years to come.

As Tim navigated the corridors of his small school, he began to demonstrate qualities that would later define his public life. His interactions with peers were marked by a sense of camaraderie and inclusiveness. He was a leader in his own right, not through any overt assertion of authority but through a genuine ability to inspire and connect with others. Whether it was organizing a game of baseball or leading a group project, Tim's leadership emerged from his willingness to listen, collaborate, and guide.

The transition from childhood to adolescence brought with it a growing awareness of the world beyond West Point. Tim's aspirations began to take shape, fueled by a blend of ambition and a desire to make a meaningful impact. The small-town environment, while nurturing, also created a backdrop for dreams that extended far beyond its borders. Tim's growing awareness of societal issues and his burgeoning interest in public service were reflections of a deeper, intrinsic drive to effect change.

The decision to attend Chadron State College marked a pivotal moment in Tim's life. The move from the familiar landscape of West Point to the more dynamic environment of Chadron was both exhilarating and challenging. Chadron, with its blend of tradition and modernity, offered Tim a new stage on which to explore his interests and ambitions. The college's setting in the Nebraska Panhandle, with its rolling hills and expansive views, was a contrast to the flatlands of his youth but equally inspiring in its own right.

At Chadron, Tim's academic pursuits took center stage. He immersed himself in the study of social science, a field that resonated deeply with his desire to understand and address societal issues. The classroom became a forum for intellectual exploration, where Tim's insights and enthusiasm enriched discussions. His professors, recognizing his potential, encouraged his growth and provided guidance that would shape his future endeavors.

Tim's time at Chadron was not confined to the classroom alone. His engagement with campus life showcased his leadership and commitment to community. Whether it was participating in student government or engaging in debates, Tim's presence was a testament to his ability to connect with others and articulate his vision. His involvement in these activities was not merely an extension of his academic pursuits but a reflection of his dedication to public service and civic engagement.

As graduation approached, Tim faced a crossroads that would determine the trajectory of his career. The decision to enlist in the U.S. Army was a reflection of his deep sense of duty and his desire to serve his country. The transition from the academic environment of Chadron to the rigorous demands of military training was both demanding and transformative. Tim embraced the challenges of Army life with the same enthusiasm that had characterized his previous endeavors. The discipline, resilience, and leadership skills developed during this period would become integral to his future career in public service.

Tim's military service was marked by a profound sense of purpose and an appreciation for the sacrifices made by those in uniform. The experiences he gained during this time provided him with a broader perspective on leadership and service.

The bonds he formed with fellow soldiers and the challenges he faced in the field contributed to his growth as a leader, preparing him for the complexities of a future career in politics.

Upon completing his military service, Tim returned to civilian life with a renewed sense of purpose. His transition to a career as a high school social studies teacher in Mankato, Minnesota, marked the beginning of a new chapter. The classroom became a stage for Tim to showcase his passion for education and his commitment to fostering a positive learning environment. His approach to teaching, characterized by enthusiasm and dedication, made him a respected and beloved figure in the Mankato community.

Tim's involvement in local community activities further demonstrated his commitment to public service. His active participation in civic initiatives and his advocacy for local issues reinforced his belief in the power of grassroots advocacy. The decision to run for public office was a natural extension of his dedication to making a difference on a larger scale. Tim's campaign for the U.S. House of Representatives was a reflection of his vision for positive change and his commitment to addressing the needs of his constituents.

Running for office presented its own set of challenges, but Tim approached the campaign with the same determination and enthusiasm that had characterized his previous endeavors. His ability to connect with voters on a personal level and his genuine commitment to addressing their concerns contributed to his success. The campaign was a testament to Tim's ability to turn his experiences and values into a compelling vision for the future.

The journey from the fields of West Point to the campaign trail was a testament to Tim Walz's unwavering commitment to public service. His story, marked by growth and transformation, is a reflection of his dedication to making a meaningful impact in the lives of others. As Tim prepared to embark on his new role in Congress, he carried with him the lessons and values that had shaped his journey—lessons that would continue to guide him as he faced new challenges and embraced new opportunities.

Chapter 2

Breaking New Ground

The transition from the familiar embrace of West Point to the expansive realm of Chadron State College marked a defining shift in Tim Walz's life. West Point, with its unchanging landscape and close-knit community, had been the crucible in which Tim's character was forged. Now, as he stepped onto the Chadron campus, he was greeted by a landscape teeming with possibilities and challenges. The Nebraska Panhandle offered a stark contrast to the flat fields of his youth—a new terrain where Tim's ambitions could take root and grow.

Chadron State College, nestled amidst the rolling hills and wide skies of northwestern Nebraska, represented a world brimming with opportunity. The campus, with its blend of historic buildings and modern facilities, provided a setting that was both stimulating and invigorating. For Tim, the transition from the tranquility of his rural hometown to the dynamic environment of Chadron was both exciting and overwhelming. The vibrant energy of the campus mirrored his burgeoning enthusiasm for higher learning.

Tim's academic journey at Chadron was marked by a profound engagement with his studies. The social science department, with its array of courses and distinguished faculty, became the heart of his intellectual exploration. Tim's natural curiosity and analytical mind found fertile ground in the rigorous curriculum. His professors, recognizing his potential, encouraged him to delve deeper into the complexities of societal structures and issues. Tim's academic prowess was evident in his thoughtful contributions to class discussions and his ability to connect theoretical concepts with real-world applications.

The classroom experience at Chadron was more than just a series of lectures and assignments; it was a forum for Tim to explore his burgeoning interest in public service. His coursework in political science and sociology provided a foundation for understanding the mechanisms of governance and the nuances of social dynamics. Tim's engagement with these subjects was not merely academic; it was fueled by a deep-seated desire to make a difference. He saw in his studies a blueprint for addressing the challenges facing society and was eager to apply his knowledge to effect positive change.

Outside the classroom, Tim immersed himself in the vibrant life of the campus. His involvement in student government and various campus organizations showcased his leadership abilities and commitment to community. Tim's role in student government was marked by a blend of vision and pragmatism. He tackled issues ranging from campus policies to student services with a blend of enthusiasm and strategic thinking. His efforts to improve the student experience and his advocacy for student needs earned him respect and admiration from his peers.

Tim's leadership extended beyond formal roles. He was a familiar face at campus events, his presence marked by an infectious energy and a genuine interest in connecting with others. Whether organizing charity events, participating in debates, or engaging in informal discussions, Tim's ability to inspire and engage was evident. His interactions with fellow students were characterized by a blend of empathy and assertiveness, traits that would serve him well in his future political career.

The academic and extracurricular experiences at Chadron were instrumental in shaping Tim's vision for his future. The combination of rigorous coursework, leadership opportunities, and community involvement provided him with a multifaceted understanding of the world. Tim began to envision a career that would allow him to combine his passion for social science with his desire to serve his community. His experiences at Chadron solidified his commitment to public service and laid the groundwork for his future endeavors.

As graduation approached, Tim faced the pivotal decision of how to channel his passions and skills into a career. The world beyond Chadron was a realm of infinite possibilities, and Tim was determined to find a path that would allow him to make a meaningful impact. His experiences at Chadron had prepared him for this next chapter, equipping him with the knowledge, skills, and vision necessary to navigate the complexities of a career in public service.

The decision to enlist in the U.S. Army was a significant turning point in Tim's life. The Army offered a unique opportunity to serve his country while further developing his leadership abilities. The transition from the academic environment of Chadron to the disciplined life of a soldier was both challenging and transformative. Tim approached this new phase with the same enthusiasm and determination that had characterized his previous endeavors.

Military training was a rigorous and demanding experience, one that tested Tim's physical endurance and mental resilience. The discipline and structure of Army life were a stark contrast to the relative freedom of college, but Tim embraced the challenge with a commitment to excellence. The lessons learned in the Army—lessons in leadership, teamwork, and perseverance—would become integral to his future career in public service.

Tim's military service was marked by a profound sense of duty and a deep appreciation for the sacrifices made by those in uniform. His experiences in the field provided him with a broader perspective on leadership and service. The bonds he formed with fellow soldiers and the challenges he faced during his service contributed to his growth as a leader. These experiences prepared him for the complexities of a future career in politics, where the skills and values honed in the Army would be crucial.

Upon completing his military service, Tim returned to civilian life with a renewed sense of purpose. His transition to a career as a high school social studies teacher in Mankato, Minnesota, marked the beginning of a new chapter. The classroom became a stage for Tim to showcase his passion for education and his commitment to fostering a positive learning environment. His approach to teaching, characterized by enthusiasm and dedication, made him a respected and beloved figure in the Mankato community.

Tim's role as a teacher was not merely a profession but a calling. His ability to connect with students and inspire them to reach their full potential was evident in his interactions with them. Tim's classroom was a place where students felt valued and encouraged to explore their interests. His teaching methods, grounded in a deep understanding of social science and a genuine concern for his students' well-being, created an environment conducive to learning and personal growth.

Outside the classroom, Tim's involvement in local community activities further demonstrated his commitment to public service. His active participation in various civic initiatives and his advocacy for local issues underscored his belief in the power of grassroots activism. Tim's engagement with community organizations and his efforts to address local needs reinforced his dedication to making a difference in the lives of others.

The decision to run for public office was a natural progression for Tim. His experiences as a teacher and community advocate had provided him with a deep understanding of the issues facing his constituents. He saw an opportunity to make a meaningful impact on a larger scale, using his skills and knowledge to contribute to the policy-making process. Tim's campaign for the U.S. House of Representatives was a reflection of his commitment to public service and his desire to effect positive change.

Running for office presented its own set of challenges, but Tim approached the campaign with the same determination and enthusiasm that had characterized his previous endeavors. His ability to connect with voters on a personal level and his genuine commitment to addressing their concerns were key factors in his success. The campaign was a testament to Tim's ability to turn his experiences and values into a compelling vision for the future.

The journey from Chadron State College to the campaign trail was a testament to Tim Walz's unwavering commitment to public service. His story, marked by growth and transformation, is a reflection of his dedication to making a meaningful impact in the lives of others. As Tim prepared to embark on his new role in Congress, he carried with him the lessons and values that had shaped his journey—lessons that would continue to guide him as he faced new challenges and embraced new opportunities.

Chapter 3

Rising Through the Ranks

Tim Walz's entry into the arena of public service was not merely a shift in career but a profound transformation of purpose. As he stepped away from the military and into the classroom, the landscape of Mankato, Minnesota, became the canvas upon which he would craft his new role. Mankato, with its vibrant community spirit and bustling civic life, offered a setting ripe for Tim's continued evolution as a leader and advocate. His journey from a soldier to a high school teacher was marked by a seamless integration of his past experiences with his present aspirations.

Mankato, with its mix of historic charm and contemporary growth, presented a contrast to the disciplined world of military life. The city, with its welcoming streets and active community, was a place where Tim could channel his energies into nurturing the next generation. The transition from the structured environment of the Army to the dynamic atmosphere of a high school classroom was both invigorating and challenging. Tim embraced this new role with the same dedication and fervor that had characterized his military service.

The high school classroom became Tim's new battleground, where he wielded the tools of education to shape young minds. His approach to teaching was both innovative and compassionate, reflecting his belief in the transformative power of education. Tim's classroom was more than a space for academic instruction; it was a nurturing environment where students were encouraged to explore, question, and grow. His lessons extended beyond the textbook, incorporating real-world issues and fostering critical thinking skills. The respect he commanded from students and colleagues alike was a testament to his genuine commitment to their success.

Tim's teaching style was characterized by a deep engagement with his students. He approached each lesson with enthusiasm, infusing his curriculum with relevance and dynamism. His ability to connect with students on a personal level created an atmosphere of mutual respect and trust. Tim's presence in the classroom was marked by an infectious energy, a quality that inspired his students to participate actively and think deeply about the subjects at hand.

Beyond the classroom, Tim's involvement in the Mankato community further underscored his commitment to service. His engagement with local organizations and civic initiatives highlighted his belief in the importance of grassroots advocacy. Tim was a familiar face at community events, his participation marked by a genuine desire to contribute positively to the lives of others. Whether it was volunteering at local charities, participating in town hall meetings, or supporting local causes, Tim's presence in the community was a reflection of his dedication to making a difference.

The decision to run for public office emerged from Tim's experiences as a teacher and community advocate. His involvement in local issues and his understanding of the challenges facing his constituents provided him with a unique perspective. The campaign for the U.S. House of Representatives was a natural extension of his commitment to public service. Tim's candidacy was not merely a bid for political office but a continuation of his lifelong dedication to effecting positive change.

Running a campaign was a formidable challenge, but Tim approached it with a blend of strategic thinking and grassroots enthusiasm. His ability to connect with voters on a personal level was a key factor in his success. Tim's campaign was characterized by a focus on listening to constituents, understanding their concerns, and presenting solutions that resonated with their needs. His approach was both pragmatic and empathetic, qualities that endeared him to voters and set him apart from his competitors.

The campaign trail was a whirlwind of activity, characterized by speeches, debates, and countless interactions with voters. Tim's ability to navigate the complexities of the political landscape was a testament to his skills as a communicator and leader. He engaged with the electorate in a manner that was both authentic and compelling, effectively conveying his vision for the future and his commitment to addressing the issues facing his district.

The success of Tim's campaign was a reflection of his ability to mobilize support and build connections within the community. His victory in the election was not merely a personal achievement but a testament to the power of grassroots advocacy and the impact of dedicated public service. As he prepared to take on his new role as a member of Congress, Tim carried with him the lessons and experiences that had shaped his journey thus far.

Tim's arrival in Washington, D.C. marked the beginning of a new chapter in his public service career. The transition from local to national politics was both exciting and challenging, presenting a range of opportunities and responsibilities. Tim's approach to his new role was characterized by a commitment to representing the interests of his constituents while navigating the complexities of national legislation.

In Congress, Tim faced a range of issues that demanded both legislative expertise and a deep understanding of the needs of his district. His approach to policy-making was informed by his experiences as a teacher and community advocate. Tim's ability to balance the demands of national politics with the needs of his constituents was a reflection of his dedication to effective and responsive governance.

Tim's tenure in Congress was marked by a focus on key issues that resonated with his district. His work on education policy, healthcare reform, and veterans' affairs reflected his commitment to addressing the needs of his constituents. Tim's ability to build bipartisan support for his initiatives was a testament to his skills as a negotiator and his dedication to finding common ground.

Throughout his career, Tim Walz has demonstrated a profound commitment to public service, characterized by a blend of personal dedication and professional expertise. His journey from West Point to Washington, D.C. is a testament to his resilience, leadership, and unwavering dedication to making a positive impact. Tim's story is one of growth, transformation, and a relentless pursuit of excellence—a narrative that continues to inspire and engage those who encounter it.

Chapter 4

Navigating the Storm

Tim Walz's arrival in Washington, D.C. was not merely a physical transition from Mankato; it marked the beginning of a profound journey into the heart of national politics, a realm both exhilarating and fraught with challenges. The city, with its imposing monuments and labyrinthine bureaucracy, was a stark contrast to the familiar rhythm of small-town life. Yet, amid the grandeur and complexity of the nation's capital, Tim's resolve remained steadfast, rooted in the values and experiences that had shaped his career.

The grandeur of the Capitol, the hub of American legislative power, stood as both a symbol of democracy and a complex web of political maneuvering. Tim's entry into this world was marked by a blend of idealism and pragmatism. He entered Congress with a clear mission: to represent the interests of his constituents and to effect meaningful change on a national scale. The early days in Washington were a whirlwind of orientations, briefings, and introductions—a steep learning curve that Tim navigated with characteristic determination.

The legislative landscape was a realm of intricate procedures and fierce debates, a far cry from the straightforward demands of local politics. The halls of Congress echoed the voices of seasoned politicians, each with their agendas and perspectives. Tim, with his background in education and community service, approached this new environment with a blend of respect and resolve. He understood that to make a difference, he needed to grasp the nuances of policy-making and the intricacies of the legislative process.

One of the early tests of Tim's political acumen came with his involvement in key committees. His assignments were strategically chosen to align with his expertise and passions. As a member of the House Committee on Education and the Workforce, Tim was positioned to influence policy on issues close to his heart. The committee's discussions were a crucible of ideas, where proposals were debated, refined, and sometimes discarded. Tim's approach was characterized by a deep commitment to understanding the impacts of policy on real-world education and workforce issues. His contributions were informed by his experiences as a teacher and his dedication to improving educational outcomes.

The healthcare reform debate was another arena where Tim's influence was felt. The complexities of healthcare policy were daunting, but Tim approached the issue with the same thoroughness that had defined his previous roles. His efforts were aimed at finding common ground in a polarized environment. The healthcare system, with its myriad challenges and stakeholders, required a balanced approach— one that addressed the needs of constituents while navigating the intricacies of national policy.

Tim's work on veterans' affairs was another area where his personal experiences resonated. His military service had given him a profound understanding of the challenges faced by veterans, and he was determined to ensure that their needs were met. The work was deeply personal, driven by a commitment to honor the sacrifices made by those who had served. Tim's efforts in this domain were characterized by a relentless pursuit of improvements in veterans' benefits and support services. His work was a testament to his belief in the importance of giving back to those who had given so much.

Navigating the storm of national politics required more than just policy expertise; it demanded an ability to build alliances and negotiate effectively. Tim's approach was marked by a commitment to bipartisanship and a willingness to engage with colleagues across the political spectrum. His ability to find common ground and foster cooperation was a key factor in his success. The legislative process, with its frequent compromises and negotiations, required a delicate balance of assertiveness and diplomacy.

The challenges of public service were not confined to the legislative arena. Tim's personal life was also impacted by his new role. The demands of a congressional career were immense, often requiring long hours and frequent travel. Balancing the demands of public service with family life was a constant challenge, but Tim's commitment to his family remained unwavering. His spouse and children were a source of support and grounding, helping him navigate the pressures of his career.

The role of a Congressman also involved engaging with constituents back home. Tim's efforts to stay connected with his district were a testament to his commitment to representation. He held town hall meetings, participated in local events, and made a concerted effort to listen to the concerns of his constituents. This direct engagement was crucial for understanding the needs and perspectives of those he represented, and it helped him maintain a sense of connection to the community he served.

The media landscape was another aspect of Tim's new reality. The scrutiny and attention that came with public office required a deft handling of media relations. Tim's approach was characterized by openness and transparency, qualities that helped him build trust with both the media and the public. His ability to communicate effectively and manage public perception was an important aspect of his role, contributing to his effectiveness as a legislator.

As Tim's tenure in Congress progressed, he faced a series of legislative battles and political challenges. Each issue brought its own complexities and required a nuanced approach. Whether addressing budget concerns, navigating partisan disagreements, or advocating for specific policies, Tim's ability to remain focused on his goals and maintain his integrity was a defining feature of his career.

The pressures of national politics were tempered by moments of personal and professional fulfillment. Tim's accomplishments in Congress were a reflection of his dedication and hard work. His contributions to key legislation, his efforts to represent his constituents, and his ability to build alliances were all part of a broader narrative of public service. The successes and setbacks, the victories and challenges, all contributed to the rich tapestry of his career.

Tim Walz's journey through the storm of national politics was marked by resilience, determination, and a steadfast commitment to his values. His experiences in Congress were a testament to his ability to navigate complex issues, build meaningful connections, and effect positive change. As he continued to serve, Tim's story was one of growth, adaptation, and unwavering dedication to the principles of public service.

Chapter 5

Against the Tide

Tim Walz's tenure in Congress was a journey through a labyrinthine political landscape, marked by both significant achievements and formidable challenges. As he navigated this complex world, his resolve was tested by shifting tides and the unrelenting pressures of national politics. The halls of Congress, with their grand architecture and bustling activity, became a battleground where every decision had the potential to impact millions.

The legislative process, though often appearing as a series of well-orchestrated debates and decisions, was in reality a fraught and intricate dance. Each bill and policy proposal passed through a maze of committees, negotiations, and amendments before reaching the floor for a vote. Tim's role in this process was both a privilege and a responsibility, demanding an acute understanding of policy details and a strategic approach to legislation. His effectiveness as a legislator was defined by his ability to weave through this intricate web, balancing the competing interests of his district with the broader goals of national policy.

One of the most significant challenges Tim faced was addressing the polarized nature of contemporary American politics. The ideological divides that characterized the national discourse presented a formidable barrier to effective governance. As a centrist voice in a highly partisan environment, Tim's ability to bridge these divides was both a strength and a strategic necessity. His approach was characterized by a commitment to dialogue and compromise, seeking common ground in an era where such efforts were often met with resistance.

The debates over healthcare reform, for instance, highlighted the difficulties of navigating a deeply divided political landscape. The issue of healthcare was not just a policy matter but a deeply personal one for many Americans, each with their own experiences and expectations. Tim's efforts to address healthcare reform were marked by a careful balancing act, aiming to incorporate diverse viewpoints while striving for solutions that could garner bipartisan support. His work in this area was a testament to his belief in the importance of accessible and effective healthcare for all, as well as his ability to engage constructively with differing perspectives.

Another significant area of focus for Tim was veterans' affairs. His commitment to improving the lives of veterans stemmed from his own military service and a profound respect for those who had served. The challenges faced by veterans were multifaceted, encompassing issues ranging from healthcare to employment and mental health support. Tim's work in this field involved advocating for policies that would enhance support services and improve access to benefits. His efforts were driven by a personal understanding of the sacrifices made by veterans and a determination to ensure that their needs were met with the respect and care they deserved.

The economic landscape of the nation also posed a series of challenges and opportunities. Tim's work on economic policy was guided by a commitment to fostering growth while addressing the needs of working families. Economic legislation often involved navigating complex interests and competing priorities, requiring a nuanced approach to policy-making. Tim's focus on economic issues was characterized by an emphasis on job creation, support for small businesses, and efforts to address income inequality. His ability to engage with stakeholders and advocate for effective solutions was a key aspect of his legislative work.

As Tim grappled with these issues, he also faced the realities of political life, including the demands of fundraising and electoral strategy. The need to secure financial support for re-election campaigns was a constant presence, influencing both the day-to-day activities of his office and the broader strategic decisions he made. Tim's approach to fundraising was marked by a commitment to transparency and integrity, seeking to build support through genuine connections with constituents rather than relying on partisan divisions.

The personal sacrifices required by public office were another aspect of Tim's experience. The demands of a congressional career often meant long hours, frequent travel, and significant time away from family. Balancing the demands of public service with personal life was a constant challenge, and Tim's ability to manage these competing priorities was a testament to his dedication and resilience. His family provided a crucial source of support and grounding, helping him navigate the pressures and demands of his career.

Tim's legislative achievements, while significant, were accompanied by moments of disappointment and difficulty. The nature of politics often meant that progress came in incremental steps rather than sweeping reforms. Each victory was hard-won and each setback a reminder of the complexities and limitations inherent in the legislative process. Tim's ability to persevere through these challenges, maintain his focus on long-term goals, and continue advocating for his principles was a defining feature of his career.

Despite the difficulties, Tim's tenure in Congress was marked by a series of notable accomplishments. His work on education policy, for instance, led to significant improvements in funding and support for schools, reflecting his commitment to enhancing educational opportunities for all students. His efforts on veterans' issues resulted in increased support services and improved benefits, demonstrating his dedication to those who had served. Tim's contributions to economic policy also had a tangible impact, supporting job growth and addressing key issues of economic inequality.

Throughout his career, Tim Walz's ability to navigate the storm of national politics was a reflection of his resilience, determination, and unwavering commitment to public service. His experiences in Congress were characterized by a blend of strategic acumen, personal dedication, and a relentless pursuit of positive change. The challenges he faced were met with a commitment to finding solutions and a belief in the importance of effective governance.

Tim's story is one of navigating complexities and overcoming obstacles, driven by a deep sense of purpose and a commitment to making a difference. His journey through the halls of Congress was marked by both triumphs and trials, each contributing to a broader narrative of public service and leadership. As Tim continued to serve, his experiences and achievements reflected a career defined by dedication, resilience, and an enduring commitment to the principles of democratic governance.

Chapter 6

Echoes of Legacy

Tim Walz's time in Washington, D.C., was not merely a phase in his career but a crucible where his ideals, aspirations, and experiences were forged into a distinctive political legacy. The grandeur of the Capitol, with its majestic domes and echoing halls, bore witness to a period of intense personal and professional evolution for Walz. The challenges he faced, the victories he achieved, and the impact he made were all part of a broader narrative that reflected his commitment to public service and his dedication to the people he represented.

The legislative arena was a theater of ambition and conflict, where every proposal and policy was a reflection of deeper values and priorities. Tim Walz's approach was defined by a combination of strategic insight and genuine empathy. His work in Congress was not just about passing bills or navigating partisan disputes; it was about addressing the core issues that affected the lives of his constituents and the nation. His focus on education, healthcare, and veterans' affairs were not just policy areas but extensions of his values and experiences.

Education policy, for Tim, was deeply personal. His years as a high school teacher had given him a profound understanding of the challenges and opportunities within the educational system. His legislative efforts were driven by a belief in the transformative power of education and a commitment to ensuring that every student had access to quality learning opportunities. Tim's work in this area was marked by a focus on increasing funding for schools, improving teacher support, and addressing disparities in educational resources. His ability to navigate the complexities of education policy was a testament to his dedication and his firsthand knowledge of the classroom experience.

Healthcare reform was another area where Tim's impact was deeply felt. The issue of healthcare resonated with many Americans, and Tim approached it with a commitment to addressing both the systemic challenges and the personal stories that shaped the debate. His efforts were characterized by a focus on expanding access to care, improving the affordability of healthcare services, and addressing the needs of underserved populations. Tim's work on healthcare was not just about policy but about ensuring that every American had the opportunity to lead a healthy life.

Veterans' affairs were a particularly personal issue for Tim. His military service had given him a profound respect for those who had served, and his legislative efforts in this area were driven by a commitment to honoring their sacrifices. Tim's work on veterans' issues included advocating for improved benefits, expanding access to healthcare, and addressing the mental health needs of veterans. His efforts were a reflection of his deep understanding of the challenges faced by those who had served in the armed forces and his determination to ensure that they received the support they deserved.

The political landscape of Washington, D.C., was characterized by a series of intense debates and negotiations. Tim's ability to navigate this environment was marked by a blend of strategic acumen and personal integrity. His approach to politics was characterized by a commitment to bipartisanship and a focus on finding common ground. The challenges of working within a polarized environment were significant, but Tim's ability to build relationships across party lines and advocate for effective solutions was a testament to his skill and dedication.

The demands of public office extended beyond the legislative arena. Tim's role as a Congressman required him to engage with constituents, participate in local events, and maintain a connection with the community he served. This aspect of his role was crucial for understanding the needs and concerns of his district and for ensuring that his work in Congress was aligned with the priorities of his constituents. Tim's efforts to stay connected with his district were characterized by a commitment to transparency and accountability, as well as a genuine desire to make a positive impact on the lives of those he represented.

The pressures of political life were often accompanied by personal sacrifices. Tim's career in Congress required long hours, frequent travel, and significant time away from family. Balancing the demands of public service with personal life was a constant challenge, but Tim's ability to manage these competing priorities was a reflection of his dedication and resilience. His family played a crucial role in supporting him through the demands of his career, providing a source of stability and grounding amid the pressures of political life.

Tim's legacy was shaped by his achievements and his approach to public service. His work in Congress was marked by a commitment to addressing key issues, advocating for effective solutions, and maintaining a focus on the needs of his constituents. The impact of his efforts was felt not just in the legislative accomplishments but in the personal stories of those whose lives were improved by his work. Tim's legacy was a reflection of his dedication to making a difference and his unwavering commitment to the principles of public service.

The end of Tim Walz's tenure in Congress was not a conclusion but a transition to new opportunities and challenges. His time in Washington had been a period of significant personal and professional growth, and his experiences had shaped his approach to leadership and service. The lessons learned and the relationships built during his time in Congress continued to influence his work and his impact on the world.

As Tim moved forward, his legacy remained a testament to his dedication and his contributions to public service. The echoes of his work in Congress were felt in the policies he championed, the relationships he built, and the lives he touched. Tim Walz's story was one of resilience, commitment, and an enduring belief in the power of public service to effect positive change. His journey through the halls of Congress was a reflection of his unwavering dedication to making a difference and his belief in the importance of serving others with integrity and compassion.

Chapter 7

Reflections and Resilience

Tim Walz's journey, spanning from the local to the national stage, is a narrative woven with threads of determination, innovation, and deep-seated values. As the years progressed, his time in Washington, D.C., evolved into a period of profound self-reflection and recalibration. The evolution from a dedicated public servant to a figure whose impact would resonate far beyond the immediate confines of legislative work was both a natural progression and a testament to his resilience.

The hallowed corridors of Congress, with their storied history and dynamic energy, were not just a backdrop to Tim's work but an environment that shaped his approach to leadership. The reflection on his tenure was not merely about revisiting past achievements but about understanding the deeper currents that drove his decisions and actions. The challenges faced, the alliances forged, and the impact made were all part of a broader narrative that spoke to the essence of his public service.

Tim's ability to reflect on his experiences was marked by an honest appraisal of both successes and setbacks. The legislative victories, while significant, were not without their complexities and compromises. Each policy initiative, from education reforms to healthcare changes, was a product of intense negotiations and nuanced decision-making. The victories were celebrated, but they were also accompanied by a recognition of the ongoing work required to address the evolving needs of the constituency and the nation.

In reflecting on his accomplishments, Tim acknowledged the importance of the collaborative spirit that defined his approach. The ability to work across party lines and engage with diverse perspectives was a hallmark of his legislative strategy. His efforts to build coalitions and find common ground were driven by a belief in the power of collective action to effect meaningful change. This approach was not always easy, but it was grounded in a commitment to solving problems and achieving results that transcended partisan divides.

The personal toll of public service was another aspect of Tim's reflection. The demands of a congressional career, with its long hours, frequent travel, and intense scrutiny, required significant sacrifices. Balancing these demands with personal and family life was a constant challenge. Tim's reflections on this aspect of his career were marked by a deep appreciation for the support of his family and a recognition of the personal costs associated with a life of public service.

As Tim looked back on his tenure, there was a clear sense of satisfaction derived from the tangible impacts of his work. The improvements in education funding, the advancements in healthcare access, and the enhanced support for veterans were all part of a legacy of positive change. These achievements were not just legislative milestones but reflections of his dedication to improving the lives of individuals and communities.

The process of reflection also involved a consideration of the broader political and social context. The polarized nature of contemporary politics presented ongoing challenges, and Tim's ability to navigate this environment was a testament to his resilience and strategic acumen. The lessons learned from these experiences were invaluable, providing insights into the complexities of governance and the importance of maintaining a focus on the broader goals of public service.

Tim's resilience was evident in his approach to overcoming obstacles and adapting to new challenges. The evolving nature of national and global issues requires a dynamic and responsive approach to leadership. Tim's ability to stay grounded in his values while adapting to changing circumstances was a key factor in his continued effectiveness as a public servant.

The legacy of Tim Walz's career was not confined to the specific policies he championed or the legislative battles he fought. It was also reflected in the relationships he built, the trust he earned, and the impact he made on the lives of those he served. His story was one of dedication, perseverance, and a profound commitment to the principles of public service.

As Tim transitioned to new opportunities and challenges, the reflections on his career served as a foundation for continued growth and impact. The experiences of his time in Congress provided valuable lessons and insights that would inform his future endeavors. The ability to reflect on these experiences with honesty and clarity was a testament to his commitment to continuous improvement and his dedication to serving others.

The narrative of Tim Walz's career was one of resilience and reflection, a story of navigating complex challenges and achieving meaningful results. His journey through the halls of Congress and beyond was a reflection of his unwavering commitment to public service and his belief in the power of positive change. As he moved forward, the legacy of his work and the lessons learned would continue to shape his approach to leadership and his impact on the world.

Chapter 8

The Horizon Beyond

The sunset over Washington, D.C., cast long shadows across the Capitol as Tim Walz stood on the threshold of a new chapter in his life. The horizon, both literal and metaphorical, represented a world of untapped potential and uncharted opportunities. With the end of his tenure in Congress, Tim was poised to explore new avenues, his journey marked by both a deep reflection on the past and a forward-looking vision for the future. The transition from public office to new endeavors was a complex process, filled with both excitement and uncertainty.

Tim's departure from Congress was not just a career shift; it was a moment of profound personal and professional evolution. The achievements and challenges of his legislative career had shaped his understanding of leadership and service, and as he stepped away from the daily grind of political life, he carried with him a wealth of experience and insight. The question now was how to channel this knowledge into new ventures that would continue to make a meaningful impact.

The post-congressional landscape was one of both opportunity and challenge. Tim's extensive network of contacts, honed through years of public service, provided a solid foundation for his new endeavors. The relationships built with colleagues, constituents, and advocates were not just professional connections but part of a broader tapestry of shared experiences and mutual respect. These relationships would serve as a vital resource as he navigated the next stages of his career.

One of the primary focuses for Tim was the continuation of his commitment to public service through non-governmental avenues. The transition from a legislative role to one of advocacy and consultancy presented a unique set of opportunities. Tim's deep understanding of policy, combined with his firsthand experience of the legislative process, positioned him well to offer valuable insights and guidance on a range of issues. His work in this area was driven by a desire to continue contributing to societal progress and to leverage his expertise for the benefit of various causes.

Education remained a key area of focus. The passion that had driven his work on education policy during his time in Congress continued to fuel his efforts in the private sector. Tim's commitment to improving educational outcomes was reflected in his involvement with educational nonprofits and advocacy groups. His ability to translate his legislative experience into actionable strategies for educational reform was a testament to his dedication to the cause.

Healthcare, too, remained a critical area of engagement. The challenges of healthcare reform and the pursuit of accessible and affordable care for all were issues that Tim continued to champion. His post-congressional work included collaborations with health organizations and participation in discussions on healthcare policy. Tim's insights, shaped by his legislative experiences, were invaluable in shaping the discourse and advancing initiatives aimed at improving health outcomes.

Veterans' affairs were another area where Tim's influence continued to be felt. The commitment he had shown to supporting veterans during his congressional career was carried forward into his new role. Tim's work with veterans' organizations and his advocacy for improved services and support systems were driven by a deep-seated respect for those who had served in the military. His efforts in this area were a reflection of his ongoing dedication to ensuring that veterans received the recognition and support they deserved.

As Tim navigated these new roles, he was also exploring opportunities to contribute to public discourse through writing and speaking engagements. His experiences and insights provided a rich source of material for articles, speeches, and public appearances. The ability to share his perspectives on policy, leadership, and public service with a broader audience was an extension of his commitment to making a positive impact.

The transition from public office also offered Tim the chance to focus on personal growth and development. The demands of congressional life had left little time for personal pursuits, but the end of his tenure allowed for a renewed focus on interests and passions outside of politics. Tim's exploration of new hobbies, engagement with local communities, and dedication to personal well-being were all part of a holistic approach to life after Congress.

The support of family and friends played a crucial role in this transitional period. The balance between public service and personal life had always been delicate, and the end of Tim's congressional career provided an opportunity to reconnect with loved ones and focus on personal relationships. The encouragement and support of his family were instrumental in navigating the changes and embracing new opportunities.

Tim's story, as he looked toward the horizon, was one of continued dedication to public service and personal growth. The achievements and experiences of his time in Congress were not endpoints but foundations for future endeavors. The journey was marked by a commitment to making a difference, leveraging expertise for the greater good, and maintaining a focus on values and principles.

The horizon, in all its vastness, symbolized both the challenges and possibilities that lay ahead. For Tim Walz, the future was a canvas of potential, shaped by a lifetime of experiences and a deep commitment to serving others. As he embarked on this new phase of his life, the echoes of his past achievements and the promise of new opportunities blended into a compelling narrative of resilience, impact, and ongoing dedication to making a positive difference in the world.

Conclusion

As the sun sets on the horizon, casting long shadows over the journey of Tim Walz, the tapestry of his life reveals a pattern woven with threads of resilience, dedication, and an unwavering commitment to service. The chapters of his story, rich with experiences and achievements, paint a portrait of a man whose influence extends far beyond the confines of legislative halls and public office. His journey, marked by both triumphs and trials, reflects a legacy that continues to evolve and inspire.

Tim Walz's trajectory from a small-town educator to a prominent national leader is more than a tale of professional success; it is a reflection of his deep-seated values and an enduring commitment to making a positive impact on the world. His experiences in Congress, where he navigated the complexities of policy-making and political negotiation, were not merely about achieving legislative victories but about embodying the principles of empathy, integrity, and dedication.

The legacy of Tim Walz is not confined to the policies he championed or the legislative battles he fought. It is also reflected in the relationships he built, the trust he earned, and the lives he touched. His ability to connect with people from diverse backgrounds, to listen and respond to their needs, was a hallmark of his approach to public service. The impact of his work is seen in the tangible improvements in education, healthcare, and veterans' support, as well as in the intangible qualities of leadership and compassion that he brought to his role.

In reflecting on Tim's journey, it becomes evident that his story is one of continuous growth and transformation. The challenges he faced, the successes he achieved, and the lessons he learned all contributed to a broader narrative of resilience and perseverance. His ability to adapt to new circumstances, to embrace opportunities for personal and professional development, and to remain steadfast in his commitment to service is a testament to his enduring legacy.

The horizon of Tim Walz's life extends beyond the immediate achievements of his career. As he moves into new roles and explores new opportunities, his legacy continues to unfold. The experiences and insights gained during his time in public service provide a foundation for continued impact and influence. Whether through advocacy, consultancy, or personal endeavors, Tim's commitment to making a difference remains unwavering.

The story of Tim Walz is also a reflection of the broader themes of public service and leadership. His journey underscores the importance of dedication, empathy, and the pursuit of meaningful change. The lessons learned from his experiences offer valuable insights into the nature of leadership, the challenges of governance, and the power of perseverance.

As the final pages of this narrative are written, the legacy of Tim Walz remains a living testament to the impact of one individual's dedication to serving others. His story serves as an inspiration to those who seek to make a difference, to those who strive to lead with integrity, and to those who believe in the power of public service to effect positive change.

In the grand tapestry of history, Tim Walz's contributions are woven into a broader narrative of resilience, compassion, and commitment. His journey is a reminder of the enduring power of service, the importance of staying true to one's values, and the impact one person can have on the world. As the horizon continues to expand, Tim's legacy remains an unwritten chapter, full of potential and promise, reflecting the ongoing journey of a life dedicated to making a difference.

The

TIM WALZ

Biography

A Comprehensive Exploration of His Legacy *of*
Service, *Leadership*, and *Resilience*

John Bison

Made in United States
Troutdale, OR
10/22/2024